DEVIL...
Give Me Back My
MONEY!

DEVIL...
Give Me Back My
MONEY!

Dale M. Sides

Liberating
Publications
INCORPORATED

Published by
Liberating Publications, Inc.
PO Box 974
Bedford, VA 24523
(540) 586-2622

The scripture used throughout this study is quoted from the King James Version, unless otherwise noted. Any explanatory insertions by the author within a scipture verse are enclosed within brackets [ ].

Second edition 2004
ISBN: 1-930433-18-2

Contents

Introduction

This is the second edition of *Devil, Give Me Back My Money!* The first edition was the most popular and exciting work we have thus far produced. Why? It is fun, short, simple, and it just plain **works**. One Indian pastor had a fully-furnished house and two years' salary given to him the very weekend he first applied the principles this little book contains.

The second edition is very similar to the first, with a facelift and some amazing stories and testimonies of results. Once, in Kenya, a wrestling match occurred over a last copy of the first edition. Let's not start a war over the second, there are plenty to go around.

DEVIL, Give Me Back My MONEY!

I believe that the wealth of the wicked is laid up for the righteous (as we are told in Proverbs 13:22), because it has always belonged to the righteous, anyway. The devil just stole it from us and gave it to his kids. These are the end times and just imagine what we will be able to do for God's glory when we have the financing for it. We are not greedy, just angry.

Let's go get what belongs to us!

The Background

Nobody likes a thief. In John 10:10 Jesus said, *"I am come that they might have life, and that they might have it more abundantly."*

Did Jesus succeed? If the answer is "yes," why do people still not have the more abundant life? I have heard tremendously long, involved reasons for why people do not have the more abundant life. It may have to do with fear, unbelief, ignorance, disobedience—all those things, but the root of the cause lies in the first part of John 10:10 (the devil is a thief):

> *The thief cometh not, but for to steal, and to kill, and to destroy:*

DEVIL, Give Me Back My MONEY!

Looking at the whole gamut of history, the only plausible reason why God put mankind and the devil upon this earth together was for the purpose of man dominating the devil. He put man here, as a superior spiritual being, to subdue the devil. But after Adam sinned and lost the abiding presence of the Spirit of God, he became dominated by his senses, walked only by his senses, and transferred his dominion to Satan until Jesus came and reversed the trend. Basically, by deception the devil has made mankind think that he is bigger than they are. This is not true. He is not bigger, but he is smarter than most people—even smarter than most Christians, too.

Jesus *did* come that we could have the more abundant life. He came so we could again be given the abiding presence of the Spirit of God, and with the Spirit of God, we become superior to the devil. Ephesians chapter 3 says God had this secret plan in mind from the very beginning:

> *And to make all men see what is the fellowship of the mystery,*

> *which from the beginning of the world hath been hid in God, who created all things by Jesus Christ: To the intent that now unto the principalities and powers in heavenly places might be known by the church the manifold wisdom of God, According to the eternal purpose which he purposed in Christ Jesus our Lord:*
>
> *Ephesians 3:9–11*

God kept this mystery hidden. It was His secret battle plan. God knew Adam would fall. He even wrote the message of the coming of Jesus Christ in the stars before He ever created, formed and made Adam. God had a plan and a purpose in mind all along.

He had a purpose; He wanted to teach the devil a lesson—so that the principalities and powers in heavenly places might know by the hands of the church the manifold wisdom of God. In other words, He wanted the principalities and powers to know by experience that they had been **foiled** by a superior, omniscient, all-wise God. This was "the eternal purpose which he purposed in Christ Jesus."

God had a secret He kept concealed within Himself. Namely, **that once again people can receive the abiding Spirit of God and that every place Christians walk on the face of the earth they would once again have authority over the devil. Hallelujah!**

Bless God, by His grace through Jesus Christ, we are *not* lesser, inferior spiritual beings. We are superior spiritual beings. The devil has worked overtime through doctrines of demons to convince mankind that people are nothing more than smart animals. However, you are **more** than a smart animal, you are a spirit being, and with the abiding Spirit of God within you, you are a superior, **super spiritual** being.

The Thief

Now back to this infernal, inferior thief. What would you do if you found a midget breaking into your car to steal your CD player? You might momentarily forget that we wrestle not against flesh and blood. Nobody likes a thief, and this is the attitude we need to maintain when dealing with the devil.

Ezekiel:28 tells us that one of the reasons Lucifer was thrown out of heaven is because of his greed and merchandising:

> By the multitude of thy **merchandise** they have filled the midst of thee with violence, and thou hast sinned: therefore I will cast thee as profane out of the mountain of God: and I will

destroy thee, O covering cherub, from the midst of the stones of fire. Thine heart was lifted up because of thy beauty, thou hast corrupted thy wisdom by reason of thy brightness: I will cast thee to the ground, I will lay thee before kings, that they may behold thee. Ezekiel 28:16–17

He is a greedy thief. He tried to steal the worship from God and the actual throne of God, too (Isaiah 14:12–14). Should we be surprised to find out that he also stole the gold that God gave to mankind?

And a river went out of Eden to water the garden; and from thence it was parted, and became into four heads. The name of the first is Pison: that is it which compasseth the whole land of Havilah, where there is gold; And the gold of that land is good: there is bdellium and the onyx stone.

Genesis 2:10–12

Gold was deposited in the garden of Eden. Who had jurisdictional claims over the garden of Eden? Adam. Why did God put the gold in the garden? For Adam. Why? Because Adam was God's man. And yet, look at Ezekiel 28:

> *Thou hast been in Eden the garden of God; every precious stone was thy covering, the sardius, topaz, and the diamond, the beryl, the onyx, and the jasper, the sapphire, the emerald, and the carbuncle, and gold: the workmanship of thy tabrets and of thy pipes was prepared in thee in the day that thou wast created.*
>
> *Ezekiel 28:13*

After the devil tricked Adam, he went into the garden of Eden and stole all the gold. In reality, all the gold in the world belongs to believers in Yahweh, but the devil stole it. Then he had the audacity to offer it to Jesus if He would worship him (Luke 4:6). He actually tried to merchandise Jesus, too.

The devil was thrown out of heaven and flung to the ground for being a thief. If you threw somebody out of your house, how much would you let them take when they left? Nothing. Likewise, when the devil was cast to the ground he had nothing. Everything that he has, he has stolen from people. If the thief was thrown out and the very next day you saw him driving a pink Mary Kay Cadillac, wouldn't you suppose he stole that, too?

People were supposed to be the devil's bosses, but now, through deception, he is stealing from them. Perhaps you have heard, "It's time to take back the land." Well, it's time to take back the gold, too!

This stuff works!

We received this teaching from an Exercising Spiritual Authority class in Atlanta, GA back in 1996. Ron had lost a $17,000 inheritance from his dad's estate. A couple years later I received over $100,000 as inheritance and paid cash for the first house we've owned.

Ron & Mary G.

The Money

There are 361 usages of the word "gold" in the Bible. The first two we found in Genesis. Over 95 percent of those 361 usages are describing the articles within the tabernacle and the temple—God's dwelling place. Do you know what that tells us, just from looking at the scope of the Word of God? All the gold belongs to God. He gave it to mankind to steward. The gold was supposed to be put into the tabernacle or the temple of God. Do you know what the temple of God is now? It is the church of the Body of Christ. The money in all the world belongs to Christianity. This is not greed; this is just the truth. All the gold in the entire world belongs to Christianity. "The earth is the LORD'S and the fullness thereof," according to Psalm 24:1. He put it here for us. The devil stole it.

DEVIL, Give Me Back My MONEY!

What if you gave your 6'1" tall strapping son his lunch money and later a puny kid, only 5'4" tall and about 130 pounds, walked up and bullied him, slapped him, and took away his lunch money. Then your son comes home crying, "Dad, go down and get it for me." What would you do? I would tell him, **"Go get it back."** I'd tell him to go down there, pick the guy up, and demand to get his money back. And if he didn't give it back, to **take it back—with interest!**

The problem is that the devil is also a deceiver. He has bullied Christians into thinking that he is more powerful than they are. If somebody won't fight, you can take everything they have. There may be a lot of things you have had taken from you that you are praying to God to get back. God does not have them and the fact is that **you** have to go get them back from the devil.

> *Beloved, I wish above all things that thou mayest prosper and be in health, even as thy soul prospereth.*   *3 John 2*

The will of God is for people to prosper and be in health. This includes more than money, but it certainly **does** include money. When Christians realize that God wants them to have money and then they don't *have* it, they have a tendency to blame God and subtly accuse Him of lying.

> But my God shall supply all your need according to his riches in glory by Christ Jesus.
> *Philippians 4:19*

Yes, God does supply our need, but a thieving midget has bullied Christians and has taken the money that God gave. The devil has caused people to be so deceived that they turn around and say, "Why doesn't God meet my needs?" The truth of the matter is: **God gave it to you and the devil stole it.** Don't blame God.

Look at the nations around the world where poverty reigns supreme. These are places where there is almost no knowledge of the Scriptures, or of Jesus Christ. Bless God, He wants this truth known to every person in the world. We will start with the money coming back to Christian believers, and then we can teach others. Then all of us can do exactly what Moses did when the children of Israel left Egypt. When they were freed from Pharoah (a figure for Satan), not only did Israel leave to go worship—but they took their rightful possessions—the gold.

I like to talk about money, because I like to talk about deliverance. Do you know how much money you need? **You need all of it that is yours.** Amen. If you didn't need it, then why did God give it to you? In addition, what about your health? Have you been afflicted in your body or in your mind? Have you been afflicted in your pocketbook? **In the name of Jesus Christ, stand up and fight! Let's take back whatever the thief has stolen!** Very quickly you will see that the money comes forth when the devil is subdued. This is war.

The Rules of War

Your money has been stolen because you are at war, and in warfare there are rules for winning. The first priority is not even to get armor or weapons, the first order of business is to get an *attitude*. You have got to *get angry* and confront the enemy.

> *Be ye angry, and sin not: let not the sun go down upon your wrath: Neither give place to the devil.*
>
> *Ephesians 4:26–27*

If you have lost your money, the "place" has been taken; you need to take back your ground.

Stand up (Ephesians 6:13). Proclaim the attitude of a warrior, and say: "I'm tired of being shot at. I'm tired of being stolen from. The devil is **not** having what is mine. I am bigger than he is. I'm taking my money back. That bully beat me up and took my lunch money. I am tired of it. I want it back. I want **all** of it back." In the name of Jesus Christ, "I want my money. I am having it back. I am not being stolen from anymore. I want my family back, my children, and my health. I'm going after it."

"Love never fails," is not a rule of warfare. It is the standard of relationship within the family of God. The rule we play by when dealing with demons and in spiritual warfare is, "All is fair in love and war." We are at war! Don't tell me love works with the devil. You don't deal with the devil by saying, "Oh please, Mr. Devil, I just love you so much, please give me back my money." You say, "In the name of Jesus Christ, you cursed liar and thief, I'm having my money. Cough it up." Love doesn't work with the devil. Remember: "All is fair in love and war."

Maybe he has stolen from your ancestors preceding you, perhaps from your Mom and Dad. Maybe your health was stolen before you were born; perhaps you were born with afflictions in your body. (That is why the disciples said, "Who did sin, this man, or his parents, that he was born blind?" See John 9:2.)

The major thing we need to realize right now is that we need to cultivate an attitude suitable for warfare, and that attitude is not love. Unless you have the proper attitude for fighting and taking a stand, it doesn't do you much good to put on the armor of God (Ephesians 6:10–18). Go ahead, put on your armor of God. Shod your feet with the preparation of the gospel of peace; put on the helmet of salvation. Then sit down and let the devil beat you in the neck and all over the back. No! Stand up and stop this madness. Let's break the cycle of intimidation. Get an attitude like Moses had.

In Exodus chapter 3, one man of God (Moses) walked into town. He had a little bit of faith and a whole lot of power and Moses backed Pharaoh right against the wall. He said to the children of Israel...

> But every woman shall borrow
> of her neighbour, and of her that
> sojourneth in her house, jewels

> *of silver, and jewels of gold, and*
> *raiment: and ye shall put them*
> *upon your sons, and upon your*
> *daughters; and ye shall spoil the*
> *Egyptians.*

> *Exodus 3:22*

The word "borrow" is the word "demand." Can you imagine them saying this? "Excuse me, would you let me borrow all your jewels—your silver, your gold? All I am doing is leaving town, walking out through the Red Sea and you will never get them back again. Could I just borrow them for the rest of your life?" No, **"Give it here,"** is what they said. "I demand it—give it here!"

Once Moses made his demands for freedom, the fight began. He had the right attitude. You need to prepare yourself, too. If you're going to quit part of the way through this, then don't start. Moses would not stop until the people were free and their money was returned.

> *And the LORD said unto Moses,*
> *Stretch out thine hand toward*
> *heaven, that there may be*
> *darkness over the land of Egypt,*
> *even darkness which may be*

felt. And Moses stretched forth his hand toward heaven; and there was a thick darkness in all the land of Egypt three days: They saw not one another, neither rose any from his place for three days: but all the children of Israel had light in their dwellings. And Pharaoh called unto Moses, and said, Go ye, serve the LORD; only let your flocks and your herds be stayed: let your little ones also go with you.

Exodus 10:21–24

Moses said, "Not so." There is another law involved in spiritual warfare: "To the victor go the spoils." We do not negotiate terms.

Pharaoh had finally said, "Okay, you can go, but leave your herds and you can take your children." But Moses said, "No, I'm not leaving without the spoils. I am taking it all. I am taking the herds, I'm taking the flocks, I'm taking the kids, I'm taking the money and I'm leaving." These are the spoils of war for the taking, once you break the strongman.

He broke the spiritual principality in Egypt and said, "I am taking it all—everything."

> *And Moses said, Thou must give us also sacrifices and burnt offerings, that we may sacrifice unto the LORD our God. Our cattle also shall go with us; there shall not an hoof be left behind; for thereof must we take to serve the LORD our God; and we know not with what we must serve the LORD, until we come thither. But the LORD hardened Pharaoh's heart, and he would not let them go. And Pharaoh said unto him, Get thee from me, take heed to thyself, see my face no more; for in that day thou seest my face thou shalt die. And Moses said, Thou hast spoken well, I will see thy face again no more.*
>
> *Exodus 10:25–29*

This record continues in chapter 11:

> *And the LORD said unto Moses, Yet will I bring one plague more upon Pharaoh, and upon Egypt;*

afterwards he will let you go hence: when he shall let you go, he shall surely thrust you out hence altogether.

Exodus 11:1

He said, "Not only is he going to let you go, but he is going to **want** you to leave." That's what God is saying here.

Speak now in the ears of the people, and let every man borrow of his neighbour, and every woman of her neighbour, jewels of silver, and jewels of gold.

Exodus 11:2

This is what Moses is telling Pharaoh. He said, "You're right, you'll not see me anymore. You'll want me to go, and we are taking all the gold, too."

And Moses said, Thus saith the LORD, About midnight will I go out into the midst of Egypt: And all the firstborn in the land of Egypt shall die, from the first-born of Pharaoh that sitteth upon his throne, even unto the firstborn of the maidservant

> *that is behind the mill; and all*
> *the firstborn of beasts. And there*
> *shall be a great cry throughout*
> *all the land of Egypt, such as*
> *there was none like it, nor shall*
> *be like it any more. But against*
> *any of the children of Israel shall*
> *not a dog move his tongue,*
> *against man or beast: that ye*
> *may know how that the LORD*
> *doth put a difference between*
> *the Egyptians and Israel.*
>
> *Exodus 11:4–7*

The angel of the Lord smote Pharaoh (a type for the devil) and spoiled him. He will do it for us just as he did it for the children of Israel. He makes a distinction between the children of God and the children of the world. The angel of the Lord fought for God's people, took the money, gave it to the children of Israel and they walked out of town loaded with gold.

> *And all these thy servants shall*
> *come down unto me, and bow*
> *down themselves unto me,*
> *saying, Get thee out, and all the*
> *people that follow thee: and*

after that I will go out. And he went out from Pharaoh in a great anger.

Exodus 11:8

Moses barked in Pharaoh's face and you will have to bark in the devil's face, too. Moses said, "You are exactly right. You are not going to see me again. The next time, you are going to want me to leave. It's over. You are going to lose the first-born of everything you have. We are taking the gold and we're leaving. You are going to kick us out because you don't want us to stay." Know why? "To the victor go the spoils."

And Pharaoh rose up in the night, he, and all his servants, and all the Egyptians; and there was a great cry in Egypt; for there was not a house where there was not one dead. And he called for Moses and Aaron by night, and said, Rise up, and get you forth from among my people, both ye and the children of Israel; and go, serve the LORD, as ye have said. Also take your flocks and your herds, as ye have said, and be gone; and bless me also. And the Egyptians were urgent upon the people, that they might send them out of the land in haste; for they said, We be all dead men.

Exodus 12:30–33

How about David?

Moses was not the only warrior who spoiled the devil. How about King David? Do you know why Israel rose to the prominence that they did under David's leadership? David was a man after God's own heart. He was a warrior!

It makes sense, doesn't it? God doesn't have your money. God has never had your money. God blessed you when He gave you the ability to get wealth (Deuteronomy 8:18). It's just that a bully has taken your lunch money from you. Well, I hope you get mad. "Be ye angry and sin not" is a command in the Word of God (Ephesians 4:26a). It says to get angry. Get good and hot. Just don't sin when you get angry. David understood this well and carried it out.

And David took the shields of gold that were on the servants of Hadadezer, and brought them to Jerusalem.

2 Samuel 8:7

David knew the rule of warfare, "To the victor go the spoils." Every time they beat up on a country, they went in and took all their gold. Well, every time Israel got beat up, the devil took it from them. The Philistines took the ark of the covenant out of the tabernacle, too. "To the victor go the spoils." It's spiritual warfare. Verse 11 talks about all the things which David brought back with him:

Which also king David did dedicate unto the LORD, with the silver and gold that he had dedicated of all nations which he subdued.

2 Samuel 8:11

"Subdued" means "conquered." This is what Adam was supposed to do, to subdue the world. This is what Moses and David did, and what you must do.

How about David?

Look at Job. God gives instructions to Job and then He says,

> *Then will I also confess unto thee that thine own right hand can save thee.*
>
> *Job 40:14*

The right hand is the hand of authority. God told Job to stand up and claim what was rightfully his. The devil had stolen it—stole his health, stole his family, stole his money, stole everything. He said, "You can get it back, Job. If you'll stand up and take it." It's all about spiritual warfare. Job had forfeited his authority.

Maybe you have forfeited *your* authority. Maybe you've been deceived, too. Thank God for forgiveness, and thank God for proper instruction. Now that you know better, you can do better.

Bless God, the truth is out. "The secret things belong unto the Lord, our God," (Deuteronomy 29:29) until they are revealed unto mankind. **The devil's got your money. The devil's got your health. The devil's got your family. Take it back!**

DEVIL, Give Me Back My MONEY!

In the name of Jesus Christ, take it back. Command, "Give it back, devil! Give it back. Give it back. I'm having what's mine!"

A Testimony of Deliverance

After hearing "Devil Give Me Back My Money!" taught in Virginia last August, Dana and I began to command in the spirit realm, that the devil give us back our money and the angels of God fight for us and deliver our money. We would do this every morning around seven o'clock. And during my 30 minute drive to work in the evening I would specifically command that the devil get away from my Dad and his properties. I would release angels to protect him. My Dad had a piece of property that he had been trying to sell since 1993. Many people were interested over the years, but they could never get their loans approved. In mid-September, my Dad told me that his property sold for nearly $80,000 and will close in late October. To my surprise, he also told me that he's giving the money in equal protions to my brother, two sisters and myself. Praise God our Father and His Son Jesus!

Rick & Dana R.

A Vision

Awhile back I was sleeping at about 12:45 in the morning and all of a sudden I had a revelation dream. It was just like an open vision, but it happened at night, so we'll call it a dream. This was a full-fledged open vision, and I was totally engulfed in it. (Paul experienced something like this when he was taken to Paradise, as 2 Corinthians 12 speaks of.)

In the vision, I walked in the door of a bank. As I walked down the hallway, ahead of me was the bank vault. The vault door was open, so I walked right into it. Wouldn't you?

The Lord then spoke to me and said, "You know where you are, don't you?" I responded and said, "Yes, Sir, I do. I am in the devil's bank vault." He said, "You're right. That's exactly where you are. And I have the key." He then said, "You figured out how to get in by exercising your authority over the devil."

I looked around on the floor of the vault and there were boxes tied with twine. On each box was a three-by-five card. Written on each card was a person's name and Ephesians 1:3, "Blessed be the God and Father of our Lord Jesus Christ, who hath blessed us with all spiritual blessings in heavenly places in Christ."

The Lord said to me, "You know what these are, don't you?"

"Yes, Sir, I do. These are the blessings of God that the devil has stolen."

He said, "That is exactly right."

They were lying all over the floor. Most of them were about the same size; some a little bigger, some a little smaller.

He said, "You have been right in what you have been teaching." (I had already been sharing some of this information.)

But He also corrected me, because I had said something in error in one of the classes I had been teaching. I had said,

"Don't worry, when I break into the devil's strongbox and I see anything in there that belongs to you, I'll bring it out." But the Lord straightened out my theology. He said, "You can't bring it out for people. They must come and get it for themselves. But you can tell them where it is, and you can tell them how to get it."

In retrospect that makes so much sense, because it involves claiming your own authority. As God said to Job, and this applies to you, "By your own right hand you can save yourself." Boldly reclaim your own authority. We have been praying to God, asking for these things, yet God's instruction is for you to go slap the bully and take them back yourself. You are a super spiritual being. **Claim** your authority. Tell the devil to take his hands off your money. Tell him to take his hands off your marriage, off your life. Tell him to take his hands off your throat. In fact, put your hands on **his** throat. See how he likes it.

**Bless the Lord,
ye his angels,
that excel in
strength,
that do his
commandments,
hearkening
unto the voice
of his word.**
Psalm 103:20

The Angels

Angels are ministering spirits that minister **for** you—to make your enemies your footstool (Hebrews 1:13–14). In the spirit realm they excel in strength (Psalms 103:20) and they encamp round about you (Psalm 34:7) to guard your perimeter and to advance your position against the enemy.[1] They play a major role in getting your money back from the devil; they are the warriors and couriers. They are heavenly spirits ministering for you in spiritual warfare. The results of their wrestling in the spirit realm are manifested in the physical realm.

> *But to which of the angels said he at any time, Sit on my right hand, until I make thine enemies thy footstool?*
>
> *Hebrews 1:13*

This is talking about spiritual warfare. Notice that making your "enemies thy footstool" is set in the context of the angels. About these angels, the next verse says,

> *Are they not all ministering spirits, sent forth to minister [f-o-r] for them who shall be heirs of salvation?*
>
> *Hebrews 1:14*

Angels minister for you. They are ministering spirits sent to minister *for* you. They ministered unto Jesus in the wilderness. And they will minister to you your need.

What are all the angels doing? According to Revelation 5:11 (and Daniel 7:10), there are "ten thousand times ten thousand, and thousands of thousands" of angels. Do you know how many that is? Literally that is about 100 trillion (or more). Hebrews 12:22 says there is "an innumerable company of angels." Regardless of the exact number, you have considerable resources available to help you. These are ministering spirits. They effect changes in the spirit realm and as a result, cause things to happen in the physical realm.

Angels enter into this warfare by inter-acting with principalities and powers, the fallen angels assigned to carry out the devil's three-fold assault: to steal from, to kill, and to destroy you. When you operate the keys to the Kingdom (Matthew 16:16–19), you loose angels into battle and they bind principalities, powers and demons that have blocked or diverted the flow of your resources.

Isn't it interesting that principalities and powers are in the heavenly realm (Ephesians 3:10; 6:12), and this is exactly where your blessings are as well (Ephesians 1:3)?

The tenth chapter of Daniel reveals the battle that developed between the angel-ic host when Daniel prayed. He prayed and fasted for 21 days until a messenger (angel) got through. He did not have the name of Jesus to use, but we do. When we pray in the name of Jesus Christ, it may be possible for the angel to break through immediately—maybe not. Start with being faithful for 21 days. Angels *will* show up with your bounty if you persist.

DEVIL, Give Me Back My MONEY!

A Breakthrough Testimony

My wife and I were in need in the fall of 1999, having moved to a new locale only a few months before. I had recently left my job in favor of self-employment and work was slow; my wife was between jobs as well. We had applied the principles in *Devil, Give Me Back My Money* before with some success, but had never really zealously pursued them to the point of breakthrough. I had even taught these principles to others both in the United States and abroad. We decided that we would proclaim several times a day, together whenever possible. In addition, we invited friends to our home who wanted to see a breakthrough in this area. The daily sessions were intense, with small groups of people individually and collectively demanding their money (and other things stolen from them) back from the devil. Results did not come immediately but we were focused and determined to overcome.

After several weeks of faithful declaration we saw the fruit of our efforts. Work increased for me, my wife got a job, and we received a $5000 gift in the mail followed by another $5000 gift about 60 days later. Hallelujah! We have received more money in the form of gifts when applying *Devil, Give Me Back My Money* than at any other time.

Tim K.

Perspectives of Money

Oftentimes people want money for the wrong reasons, and even dispatch angels to bring it back for them for selfish reasons. We do need money to acquire physical things, but it is intended for physical things that can be used for "Kingdom business." God is looking to see if you will be more concerned about building His Kingdom, or your own.

Money is physical, but God requires that we be good stewards of things He has given us. So, the problem with money is not money itself; the problem is the **love** of money. In spiritual warfare, the devil works people over to think they are merely physical beings, and then, because they think they are physical beings, they want physical pleasures, and physical things. This is a very treacherous snare for wealthy people. No one can afford to be deceived.

This is spiritual warfare.[2] When the money starts coming, when you start sending ministering spirits out to bring it back, the devil starts working on your greed. He is not that strong, but he is smart. He is a tempter, and he's a deceiver. He will send the spirit of Balaam (Revelation 2:14) to wrap his fingers around your mind. He will make you think money is such a big deal and will attempt to merchandise you with it.

Many times a reference is made about the spirit of Jezebel from Revelation 2:20. Yet there is another spirit named in Revelation 2:14, called the spirit of Balaam.[3] This evil spirit is a bribery spirit that buys your allegiance and commitment to God. Actually, it causes you to "merchandise the church" for personal gain, like Balaam tried with the children of Israel (Numbers 22).

When dealing with money, tithing quells the spirit of Balaam. The spirit of Balaam tries to kill a church through starvation, like Jezebel does through manipulation and control. The spirit of Balaam says, "Tithing is not in the New Testament." That's a lie; it's in the book of Hebrews, and that is in the New Testament. It also says, "I can't afford to tithe." Statements like these are a sure manifestation of that demon. For those who say, "Well, I am not under the law of tithing," I say, "That's fine, don't be under the law of prosperity, either. They both work together, hand in hand."

Would you mind paying a tenth if you had seven times more money than you do now? Most folks would say, "Oh yes, we would be glad to give a tenth, then." Well, I'll tell you how to start the ball rolling. Send the ministering spirits out to bring more money back to you. (Angels minister for those who are about Kingdom business.) Start paying at least your tithe now. That's going to get the fingers of the devil off your brain by cursing the spirit of whoredoms and the spirit of Balaam.

Nevertheless, the Lord wants you to be prosperous. Look at the men of God in the Old Testament. Look at a few of God's wealthy men: Job, Abraham,

David, and Solomon. There was nothing wrong with them being wealthy. That was, in fact, God's provison for them.

Why else would God give Adam gold? He knew Adam was going to need gold to finance the campaign of subduing the devil. That is what money is for. It's not for hoarding, sticking it in your socks, sitting around, worrying about getting old and dying at a decrepit age of a dastardly disease. In the name of Jesus Christ, get your money back, and get your vision up—properly aligned in the will of God. For God's sake, for Jesus Christ's sake, and for the ministry's sake, we need to win people for the Lord Jesus Christ. That's what our **need** is—and why we need **all** of our money.

Develop the right perspective of money. Use it to build the Kingdom of God. By God's mercy and blessing, be wealthy. Be prosperous. Be liberal. Be obedient. Pay your tithe. Remember, you can't take it with you, but you can "wire it ahead."

Examples

I once taught this information to a hard-working couple in Virginia. The day after they went home, the husband and his wife stood in the middle of their living room floor and commanded, in the name of Jesus Christ, "Devil, give me back my money, and we send out ministering spirits to the north, east, south, and west. Bring me my money." The next day they received $1,500 in the mail, not even knowing where it came from.

To these folks, this is a lot of money (especially because the husband needed that much money to buy a truck for his business). Having the proper perspective of money, he paid his tithe and stewarded the money for "Kingdom business." The $1,500 together with what he already had gave him $3,200.

Soon afterwards, he saw a truck for sale and asked, "Lord, is that my truck?" The Lord answered, "That is your truck." He went back home to his wife and prayed about the truck. He said, "Honey, that's my truck. I only have $3,200 but I am going to get that truck, because I need it to build my business for the Lord."

He got some believers together to pray and commanded the truck to come to him. He went to see the owner who was asking $3,800 for the truck. He placed the $3,200 on the hood of the truck and said, "Mister, I'm a Christian and the Lord told me this is my truck. I have $3,200." The seller said, "I'm a deacon in the Baptist church and if the Lord told you that it's your truck, you can have it for $3,200." Thank you, God!

Another couple did this and got $75,000 two days later. A minister in India applied these principles and had a completely furnished house plus two year's salary given to him. Another minister needed money to do missionary work. He was faithful to apply these principles five times a day for a month. I found out about it when he gave me a

$1,000 tithe and said, with a big smile on his face, "This works. Not only am I going to ransack the devil's kingdom, but he's paying for it."

"Devil, give me back my money!" This does work, people. We are spiritual beings and we need this money to move our ministries. We need the physical cash to move the physical things. You may not need lots of money to be a prayer warrior, but you need some to keep food on the table to keep your body alive.

There is nothing wrong with money. I hope to God you have a **lot** of it. I hope to see you drive down my driveway with a brand new Lexus or Cadillac or Lincoln or whatever you need. But let me tell you something: If you have two of them I'm going to ask you what you're doing with the second one. You only need one. Jesus had the finest transportation in town. He got his white donkey from the Lord, but He only had one. He had the finest clothes money could buy, a seamless robe, but He only had one.

Isn't it great to serve a God that wants us to prosper? This is the revealed truth contained in the Word of God.

> *Beloved, I wish above all things that thou mayest prosper, and be in health, even as thy soul prospereth.* 3 John 2

Isn't it great to serve a God like that? God gave you all your money and said for you to give at least a tenth of it back. Invest it in spiritual matters. Wire it ahead by investing in the Bank of Paradise. Stash some cash in the spiritual futures market. Lay your rewards up in heaven. All of it belongs to God anyway, but He wants to see if you have enough spirituality to realize all of it belongs to Him by investing a tenth of it in spiritual matters. This will be the greatest return on investment you could ever possibly achieve. Jesus directed His disciples to make "secure" investments when He said,

> *Lay not up for yourselves treasures upon earth, where moth and rust doth corrupt, and where thieves break through and steal: But lay up for yourselves treasures in heaven, where neither moth nor rust*

doth corrupt, and where thieves do not break through nor steal: For where your treasure is, there will your heart be also.
Matthew 6:19–21

A Testimony of Grace

Back in 1997-98 we experienced financial hardships; our prospects were really bleak. Several people told us to file bankruptcy, but that didn't seem like the right thing to do. About that time we heard Dale Sides' teaching on Devil, Give Me Back My Money. We took it very seriously and proclaimed into the spirit realm every day, often several times a day. We told the devil to get his hands off our finances and we instructed the angels to bring back our resources. At the time we were about $150,000 in debt. We started seeing things gradually improve. At first I was working for a contractor, then it became possible for me to begin my own business. We had also learned that the riches of the world were intended for believers, so we continued to be fervent and tenacious in our proclamations.

Consistency truly paid off. The first year in business we made $600,000. The second year was $2.2 million; the third year was

DEVIL, Give Me Back My MONEY!

$3.6 million and this, our fourth year, looks like we'll come in at $5.5 million, with an outstanding profit margin (not just "getting by"). This is a testimony to God's gracious goodness. We are restoration contractors. We primarily do insurance claim repair work. Lately there have been very few calamities in our part of the country. The insurance companies are going to report great profits. But many other contractors in our field are in dire straits—either filing for bankruptcy or going out of business. We were told by a reliable source that one of our competitors presently has nine jobs. We have 67! That surely reflects God's blessings.

Recently I met with our financial advisors and was told that my situation had been the center of conversation at their firm's national meeting. I paid around $100,000 in taxes last year, and they were putting their heads together to see if anything could be done to improve my tax position. They told me that mine was a good problem (being profitable) to have—some clients have high bills and no way to meet their IRS obligation. This panel could have focused on anyone, but by the favor of God, they had devoted their time and energies to my case. I can only thank my Heavenly Father, Who is faithful to bless His children.

Verdean & Gayle L.

How to Proclaim Your Demand

Have you ever heard of making an authoritative spiritual demand? It is called a "spiritual proclamation," and it is done assertively by a recognized authority. Many examples of this are found in the Word of God. Jesus, our great example, said: "Peace, be still," in Mark 4:39; "Stretch forth thine hand," in Matthew 12:13; and "Lazarus, come forth," in John 11:43. This is the way you proclaim your money back from the devil.

First, get an *attitude*. Remember how much the devil has stolen from you and remember that when a thief is discovered he must restore seven times over (Proverbs 6:30–31). Be angry and sin not. Do not give place to the devil

(Ephesians 4:26–27), and get your rightful place of authority back from him.

Next, send the ministering spirits out! When you send the ministering spirits out, tell the devil to get his hands off your money and to give it back. Take a stand in the middle of your house. Turn to the north, the south, the east and the west and command that lying thief from hell to give back **everything** he's taken from you! Send the ministering spirits out to get it and bring it back. Make him give back seven times over! And after you do it, when the money comes, *don't forget to pay your tithe.*

When you tell the devil to get his hands off your money, **mean** it. Say it with faith. Say it loud. Shout, **"Devil, give me back my money!"** That is the way to proclaim authoritatively. Yell at the devil. The shout brought the angels to flatten the walls of Jericho. Send the ministering spirits out to go get it. There are millions and millions and millions and millions of underemployed angels. There are a lot of them, and you have a lot of money that needs to come back.

How to Proclaim Your Demand

Have you ever heard of "believing action?" Well, in this situation your proclamation is your action of faith. Did you proclaim? Then you have taken action. Have you told the devil to give you back your money? Then you have believed. Did you send out the ministering spirits? Then you have done what you needed to do. Are you paying your tithe? Are you doing what you are supposed to do? Are you working? The only believing action left to be taken is to continue to proclaim it. The action has already been taken. Instead of saying, "I'm believing," let's say, "I have believed; I have acted. It is working." Say, "It is working. It is working. It's working." Stay faithful. You'll see big results.

Do you know how much money God wants you to have? All that belongs to you. And when you get all of it back, don't forget why you have it: It is to minister physical things for spiritual beings. You need money for your ministry. There is plenty to go around. Hallelujah!

Be angry. Be spiritual. Be obedient. Be faithful. Be thankful. Send your ministering spirits out. Send them out to bring back your money. Say, "In the name of Jesus Christ, Devil, give me back my money! Ministering spirits, go bring it back. Bring it home to me. I am going to use it to move the Word of God. I am going to use it to win people for Jesus Christ in the last days."

Let's wire a bunch of it ahead to heaven in our tithes. Then when we leave, let's **do** take as much of it with us as we can. Let's leave the financial systems in disarray, confused and befuddled, when the Lord takes us off the planet. Let's leave just like Moses did. Let's make the devil **beg** us to leave. Let's take the cash, the herds, the flocks, and the booty, which is **people**. Hallelujah, hallelujah, bless God forever!

Let us raise our fists in defiance of the thief. Let us boldly proclaim:

> **"In the name of Jesus Christ, Devil, give me back my money. It is rightfully mine. I belong to God, and He gave it to me to entrust to my stewardship. You thief from hell, you stole it from**

me, and you are giving it back. Ministering spirits, go get it and bring it back. This is my abundance. I'm not asking you for it, God, because You have already given it to me. In the name of Jesus Christ I am proclaiming, Devil, give it back. Cough it up! Give it back. Ministering spirits, bring it back. I commit myself this day. As there was a willingness to perform this before, now I perform the doing of it. I'll use my resources for spiritual things. In the name of Jesus Christ, I claim this. Devil, give me back my money. Amen."

Do this faithfully—day after day and week after week. The more you need, the more you proclaim: "Devil, give me back my money!"

<u>Notes</u>

1. Dale M. Sides, *Angels in the Army* (Bedford, VA: Liberating Ministries for Christ International [LMCI], forthcoming) 13.

2. Dale M. Sides, *God Damn Satan,* (Bedford, VA: LMCI, 2000) 84–85.

3. Dale M. Sides, *The Three Doctrines of Damnation* (Bedford, VA: LMCI, 2001) 21.

Testimony Time

Our destiny restored...

It is *so* easy for the devil to steal if we don't
even know what he's doing. We had been
totally non-combative and had just let our
losses fall alongside the road. My first lesson
in "God's Finance 101" was when I realized
that my Ph.D. and MBA principles were
useless against this kind of warfare. Second,
my attitude changed from one of "doing
business my own way" to "working for The
Boss." ...We knew the Father had plans for
us, but what?

In 2001, after my wife and I heard Dale Sides
teach on "Devil, Give Me Back My Money,"
we began demanding that our past stolen
wealth be returned. We also began to
comprehend just how much the enemy *had*
stolen from us—not just in money, but in
family and "what might have been." This
knowledge about our authority to "command the return of our money" produced a

DEVIL, Give Me Back My MONEY!

very powerful attitude shift spiritually. Glenda Sue put a sign up in our office by the door which said, "Devil, give us back our money!" and together we would proclaim these words and ask angels to retrieve our stolen goods.

In May of 2002, the doors opened to partner with a brother-in-Christ in the purchase of a very profitable 24-year-old Allstate Insurance agency. Insurance agents? Residual income? Wow! We would be reaping where we had not sown. The Lord's provision brought miraculous events in finance and timing. Again and again, large sums of money were there just when we needed it. Despite overwhelming opposition, our contract to buy the agency smoothly came together, even though we didn't have insurance backgrounds. A perfect home, better than our choosing, not even on the market yet, was produced out of nowhere with the perfect financing, and is located only four minutes away from the office.

Our lives are built upon prayer and diligent service, which has transformed us into warring disciples of Jesus Christ! Our money, this house, our belongings, and even our own selves individually are His, and the devil dare not steal from the Father's own hand!

A. J. & Glenda Sue M.

An authoritative spiritual demand...

I typed up the wording from Dale's cassette ("Devil, Give Me Back My Money!") and on a regular basis I prayed first and reminded the Lord that I had not robbed Him and had tithed, and claimed blessings and authority over the power of the enemy. I said, "Principalities of the air, I demand back the money that was proportioned to me for service to my family, my church and our community! I remind you, Devil, that you were defeated at Calvary! You will bow down, get out of my way, and release my finances to me! I demand in the name of Jesus, as a spiritual authority, the right to fulfill my ministry along with the resources, revelation and relationships that I need!"

Then I spoke to the angels to go to the north, south, east and west and get my money and bring it to me, as Dale suggested. I don't know when I began, but it has been over a year. Then in April, I sent a letter to the insurance company that wanted to settle my car accident. After a couple weeks of negotiations, they sent me a check for $30,000. My massage therapist said she never heard of anyone getting more than around $5,000 for an accident similar to mine. So I'm praising the Lord for our extra funds to help us with bills! (This is the reason I could come

DEVIL, Give Me Back My MONEY!

to LMCI's Liberating Partners' Week.) Yes, God is good!

I'm still claiming the return of a car that I paid for and never drove. (I co-signed on a Town Car and never saw it, but ended up paying for the whole thing!) That was 26 years ago. Since Holly needs a car, I'm proclaiming for one!

> *For surely, O Lord, You bless the righteous, You surround them with Your favor as with a shield.*
>
> *Psalm 5:12*

Thanks, in Christ's Love.

Mary C.

Books and Booklets
by Dale M. Sides

*40 Days of Communion
in Your Home*

*Approved of God—by Grace
or by Works*

Diverse Kinds of Tongues

*Flowing in All Nine Gifts
of the Holy Spirit*

God Damn Satan

Mending Cracks in the Soul

The Anointing In & On

The Ministry of Liberality

The Three Doctrines of Damnation

*True Confessions of Spiritual
Warriors*

*Understanding & Breaking
the Schemes of the Devil*

Utilizing Gift Ministries

*You Don't Have to be Smart
to Walk with God*

*The Lord gave the word: great was
the company of those that published it.*
Psalm 68:11

Liberating Publications, Inc.
PO Box 974, Bedford, VA 24523-0974, USA
(540) 586-4074 Phone, (540) 586-9372 Fax

ORDER FORM

Qty.	Description	Price	Ext. Price
	Subtotal		
	*Sales Tax		
	S&H (See chart below)		
	Total:		

*VA residents add 4.5% sales tax.

Standard Shipping Rates	
Orders under $25.00	Add $3.95
Orders $25.01 — $75.00	Add $5.95
Orders over $75.00	Add $7.95

(Please call for expedited delivery rates.)

Name _____

Address_____

City/ST/Zip _____

Daytime Phone_____

Payment: __Check __VISA __Mastercard

Card # _____ Exp. _____

Signature: _____

(You may wish to photocopy this page for future use.)